The following artwork
was created from
2005-2008. This book
is dedicated to anyone
i swapped stories with,
bought me a beer, or
slept next to me during
this time period.

 # nce upon a time...

paintings, drawings, and tall tales by *jeremy fish*

Foreword by Aesop Rock

I would like to think that somewhere between full-blown, howling death and a basket of newborn kittens exists a climate where the malice and the mirth can mingle. A couple of daisies on your grave, a little venom in your cocoa, some broken glass in your bouncy castle. This type of polar mixer can serve as an intriguing, endlessly entertaining, true-to-life foundation from which a smidgen of lore can grow. Exaggerate the extremes even a little, and the stories, characters, and places that emerge warp accordingly. It is the recognition and exploitation of this tension that immediately drew me to the work of upstate New York-born, San Francisco-based artist Jeremy Fish.

At first glance, Fish's images seem to be rooted in an alternate world — a world where gnomes travel via saddled dachshund-back and birds of all nations hatch adorned with the heads and hairstyles of every human stereotype imaginable. The bold, precise outlines give his ideas an immediate impact, but it's the aftertaste that really cuts deep. Everything comes with a story. I have never known Jeremy to create something without a reason for it to exist and an accompanying tale. His pictures are built from the simplest ingredients, ingredients with which the everyman can identify. Fish documents his every day, every trip, every friend, and every experience within his art to the point where one could line up his life's work, decode the riddles, and have a clear idea of where he's been, how he felt about it, the types of folk he chopped it up with, and what lies ahead.

What does lie ahead? Inevitably, more days and nights locked in his oddball studio, as the "King of North Beach" maintains an awesome and inspiring work ethic. Jeremy Fish is, for all intents and purposes, the real deal. To say he works hard would be an understatement worthy of a bid in the Bog of Eternal Stench. While the public gets to soak in the varied fruits of his labor, he is laboring behind the scenes... intensely and always. The guy is an art machine fueled by coffee, beer, and the occasional well-done burger. On any given day, one can wander into Fish's studio to find an entire new body of work that did not exist one week prior, complete with a storyline as engaging as the images themselves. The output level is shocking in both quality and quantity.

But, in the end, it's all only as deep as the man behind the drafting table. In an age with fewer and fewer creative heroes worth looking up to, I can say without hesitation that, in this case, the man at the helm of the hand doing the damage is a shepherd worth following. Fish would probably cringe at a comment like that, as his hermitic and occasionally bashful composure doesn't sponge up compliments well. But, I'm writing this, so fuck him. I've been around the world and met a lot of "artists" who eat, shit, and breathe inside a bubble of self-aggrandizement, armies of yes-men at their sides ready to toot the bugles for every flimsy "breakthrough" they put forth. Jeremy Fish avoids that typecasting by boiling his intentions down to their most elemental forms: he makes pictures, he makes a lot of them, he makes them for himself, he makes them for the people, and he makes them from the heart. I am proud to say that I look up to him. You should too.

04 | first owl | 16" x 20" | 2006

buck you

64 | lost dog | 24" x 36" | 2006

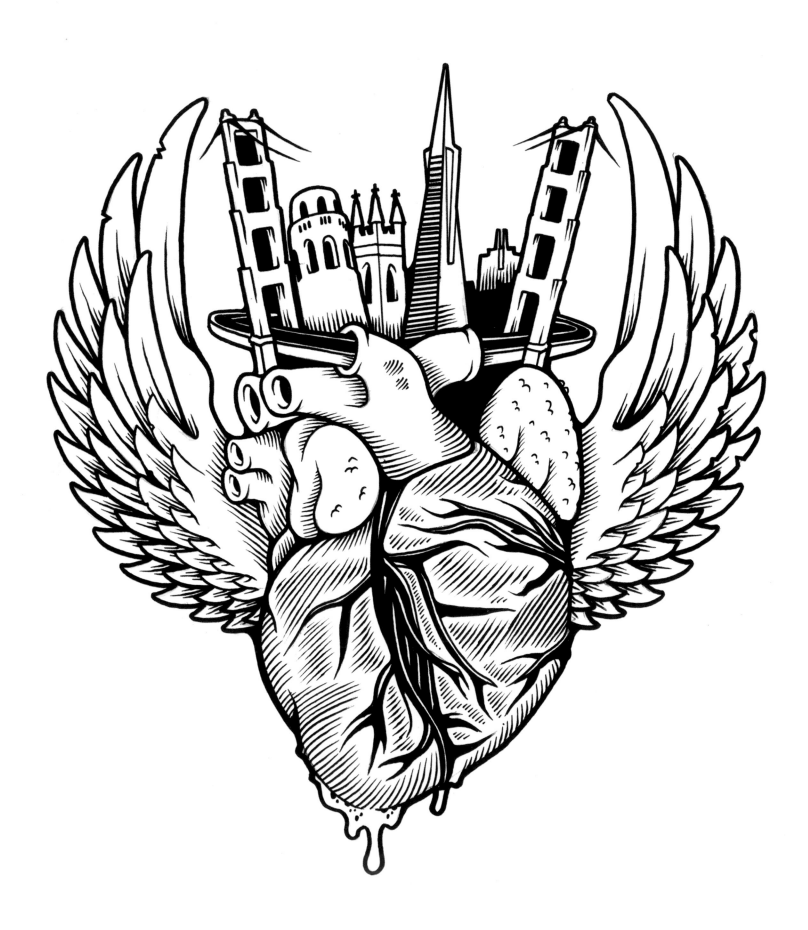

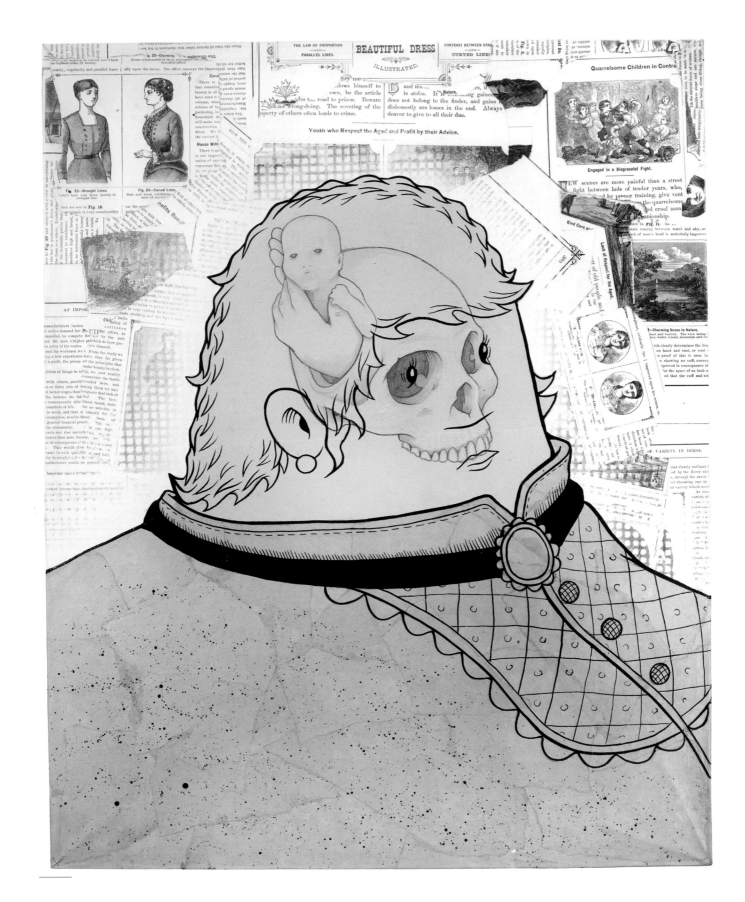

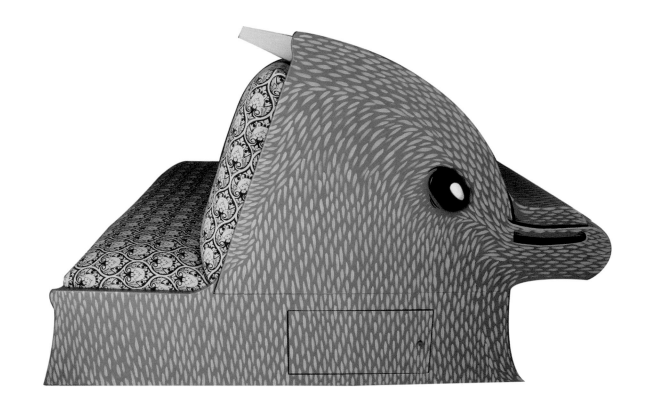

the turtle table | with Francisco Robles | 2007 | from the collection of Robin Williams | **99**

福星高照

jeremy and I became friends through skateboarding nearly two decades ago. So when he broke his ankle during a gang convention a few years back and needed some help painting a hotel room, I was glad to help

What started out as a friend working for beer has since turned into a regular gig as his assistant—which basically entails being a personal bodyguard, translator, portable entertainment system, navigator, beering aid and photographer. The following pages are brief glimpses into some of the projects we've worked on together as seen through the lens of my camera.

— Rick Marr

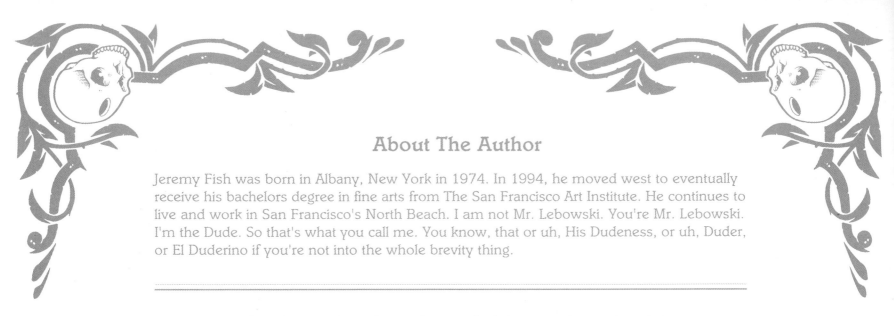

About The Author

Jeremy Fish was born in Albany, New York in 1974. In 1994, he moved west to eventually receive his bachelors degree in fine arts from The San Francisco Art Institute. He continues to live and work in San Francisco's North Beach. I am not Mr. Lebowski. You're Mr. Lebowski. I'm the Dude. So that's what you call me. You know, that or uh, His Dudeness, or uh, Duder, or El Duderino if you're not into the whole brevity thing.

Be who you are and say what you feel, because those who mind
don't matter, and those who matter won't mind.
—— Dr. Seuss

Furniture photographs by Jon Dragonette | www.dragonettephotography.com
Travel and mural photographs, and endless assistance by Rick Marr | www.laterforyou.com
All other artwork shot by Randy Dodson, and Nate Kalushner | www.open-aperture.com

www.sillypinkbunnies.com | www.superfishalsf.com | www.umbrellamarket.com
www.upperplayground.com | www.fecalface.com | www.laterforyou.com

A special thank you
to the following folks:
My team of highly skilled gnomes,
S.P.B. The almighty Silly Pink Bunnies,
my family, Rick Marr, Duane Lamb, Ian Bavitz,
Geoff Allen, Randy Dodson, Francisco Robles, Don Gamble,
The Umbrella Market, Matt Irving, John Trippe, Fecal Face.com,
Matt Revelli and the entire Upper Playground / 5024SF staff,
Cafe Trieste, Iguapop Gallery, Josh Liner Gallery, Space 1026,
White Walls Gallery, Juxtapoz, Slap Magazine, Hybrid Design
Concussion, Ordinary Kids, Dan Wolfe, Eric Noren, Whystyle
Scott Bourne and The Unbelievers (r.i.p.), Nike SB,
Skateboard Fieber.de, Nat Swope at Bloom Press,
Chance Franck and Nyoman Sedayatana,
The Big Geezers Crew, The Vapor Room,
El-P and Definitive Jux Records,
The city of San Francisco,
and all you heroes.